The Inaccurate Conception

A comedy
Richard Ahsam and Geoff Saunders

New Theatre Publications - London
www.plays4theatre.com

The edition published in 2013

New Theatre Publications

2 Hereford Close | Warrington | Cheshire | WA1 4HR | 01925 485605

www.plays4theatre.com   email: info@plays4theatre.com

New Theatre Publications is the trading name of the publishing house that is owned by members of the Playwrights' Co-operative. This innovative project was launched on the 1st October 1997 by writers Paul Beard and Ian Hornby with the aim of encouraging the writing and promotion of the very best in New Theatre by Professional and Amateur writers for the Professional and Amateur Theatre at home and abroad.

ISBN 9 781 840 94918 6

Characters

(Many can be doubled - see script)

Staff

Celia Whibley
Octavia Dutton-Griggs
Miss Belcher
Miss Cusp
Kurt Elginbrod
Mr Miller

Children (all age 7)

Jessica
Michelle
Justine
Melanie
Siobhan
Dougal
Craig
Shane
Spencer

Parents

Melindra
Dougal's Mum
Spencer's Mum
Bob
Spencer's Dad

Copyright Information

Video-Recording of Amateur Productions

Performing Licence Applications

A performing licence for these plays will be issued by "New Theatre Publications" subject to the following conditions.

Conditions

1. That the performance fee is paid in full on the date of application for a licence.
2. That the name of the author(s) is/are clearly shown in any programme or publicity material.
3. That the author(s) is/are entitled to receive two complimentary tickets to see his/her/their work in performance if they so wish.
4. That a copy of the play is purchased from New Theatre Publications for each named speaking part and a minimum of three copies purchased for backstage use.
5. That a copy of any review be forwarded to New Theatre Publications.
6. That the New Theatre Publications logo is clearly shown on any publicity material. This is available on our website.

Fees

Details of script prices and fees payable for each performance or public reading can be obtained by telephone to (+44) 01925 485605 or to the address below.

Alternatively, latest prices can be obtained from our website www.plays4theatre.com where credit/debit cards can be used for payment.

To apply for a performing licence for any play please write to New Theatre Publications 2 Hereford Close, Warrington, Cheshire WA1 4HR or email info@plays4theatre.com with the following details:-

1. Name and address of theatre company.
2. Details of venue including seating capacity.
3. Dates of proposed performance or public reading.
4. Contact telephone number for Author's complimentary tickets.

Or apply directly via our website at www.plays4theatre.com

The Inaccurate Conception
by
Richard Ahsam and Geoff Saunders

First performed as a rehearsed reading by Group 64 at the Goodrich Theatre, Putney, on 24th April 1994, with the following cast: Nick Donovan, Jill Ferguson, Paul Haken, Rowena Jones, CJ Lampard, Juanita Patrick and Warren Turner. Directed by Geoff Saunders.

Subsequently performed in a full production by Ad Hoc at Wyedean School, Chepstow, from 28th to 30th November 1996 with the following cast:

Octavia Dutton-Griggs, Melanie, Justine	*Linda Arthurs*
Celia Whibley	*Heidi Vaughan*
Miss Cusp, Siobhan, D's Mum	*Ann Llewellin*
Miss Belcher, Michelle, Melindra	*Penny Andrews*
Mr Miller, Spencer	*Chris Griffiths*
Kurt Elginbrod, Shane	*Martyn Andrews*
Elliott Strong*, Dougal, S's Dad	*William Smith-Haddon*
Craig, Bob	*Dennis Arthurs*
Jessica, S's Mum	*Jane Smith-Haddon*
"Miss Pringle at the pianoforte"	*Rosemary Griffiths*

Directed by *Penny Andrews*

* The character of Elliott Strong was removed in a later rewrite.

Characters

Staff of Verruca Street Primary School

Celia Whibley, *early 20s*
Octavia Dutton-Griggs, *headmistress*
Miss Belcher
Miss Cusp
Kurt Elginbrod
Mr Miller

Children (all age 7)

Jessica
Michelle
Justine
Melanie
Siobhan
Dougal
Craig
Shane
Spencer

Parents

Melindra, *Jessica's mother*
D's Mum
S's Mum
Bob, *Shane's father*
S's Dad

Casting

The play can be cast one-person-to-a-part, in which case the casting is M8 F12, but it is more fun to double the parts, even if this means, in some of the scenes with the children, that actors have to change characters mid-scene. The smallest cast possible is M2 F4, in which case the following casting is *suggested*:

Actress 1: Celia Whibley
Actress 2: Octavia Dutton-Griggs, Justine, Melanie, D's Mum
Actress 3: Miss Belcher, Melindra, Michelle
Actress 4: Miss Cusp, Jessica, Siobhan, S's Mum
Actor 1: Shane, Kurt, Spencer
Actor 2: Mr Miller, Bob, Dougal, Craig, S's Dad

Scene 1

An empty stage. Heavenly music. A Light comes up on Celia, C. All we see is her face, gazing upward with a mixed look of awe and fear

Voice Over Fear not, Daughter of Israel. Thy prayer has been heard. The Lord is with thee. Blessed be the young woman. I have been sent unto thee by the one God to deliver unto thee news that shall be hailed from the highest mountain to the deepest valley. For it has been written that one shall be chosen. Blessed is the one. From thee will behold the greatest and your name will be spoken until the end of time. You are the chosen.

(The lights come up further to reveal Octavia, in her full headmistress regalia, standing beatifically behind Celia. The rest of the staff — Kurt, Mr. Miller, Miss Cusp and Miss Belcher — are ranged to either side like angels.)

Octavia My dear, it's your big chance. You've been with us, what is it...?

Celia Two years, Mrs Dutton-Griggs.

Octavia Heavens, child, call me Octavia! Two years, eh? And do you feel you've grown in that time?

Celia Actually, I've lost weight a bit...
(The 'Angels' smirk.)

Octavia No! What I mean is, do you feel you've grown as a person, spiritually? Is your personality developing?

Celia I'm not sure I'm the person to answer that, really.

Octavia Well, I am. I am that person. And I say you're ready. Yes, you, Celia Whibley, look most positively ready to me.

Celia Ready, Mrs Dutton-Griggs... Octav...?

Octavia For the challenge of challenges! *(The Angels gasp.)* The task of tasks! *(The Angels gasp louder.)* The personal development opportunity of personal development opportunities! *(The Angels are all tense with excitement.)* Have you guessed yet?

Celia I'm so sorry, Mrs... Angels.

Octavia Celia!

Celia Octavia. I'm so sorry. I have no idea.

Cusp Oh, go on, guess...

Belcher We've all been through it...

Mr Miller It's not hard, girl!

Kurt Go on, guess; it's easy...

Celia Lunchtime supervision?

(The Angels break into a mirth hideous to behold.)

Octavia Please! *(The Angels instantly subside.)* My dear, I shall tell you. I am entrusting to you a vital and prestigious task.

Celia Oh, golly...

Octavia Yes, indeed, golly, yes, golly indeed. My dear, it's your turn to produce the school Nativity play!

(The Lights snap up full. Octavia retreats slowly backwards and the Angels close in on Celia, smiling with blatantly false sincerity.)

Cusp Of course, you'll get every support from us, dear...

Belcher You won't be alone, we're all here to help when you need us...

Cusp/Belcher Reach out... we'll be there!

Celia Thank you!

Cusp No problem, dear.

Belcher:

Mr Miller We stick together when things need to be done here, you know.

Kurt You can count on us in your time of need.

Mr Miller/Kurt Just let us know!

Celia Thank you.

Mr Miller/Kurt That's all right, matey!

Octavia *(booming from the back)*. So, my dear... I'll leave that to you!

Voice Over For it has been written that one shall be chosen. And from the wilderness that one will be praised. Blessed is the one. Heaven be praised.

(The lights snap to a spot on Celia. Her face twists into a silent scream. The lights cross-fade to:)

Scene 2

The classroom. Celia faces the class (all except SPENCER)

Celia   *(to us).* Celia Whibley, twenty-four, two years out of teacher training college (B.Ed Honours, you know) is nearing the end of a trying day with class 3C at Verruca Street Church of England Primary School. *(To the class.)* Well, 3C, I've got some good news for all of you..Michelle.

Shane   You're leaving!

Celia   No, Shane, I'm not. I'd miss your charm and politeness too much. No, it's something really exciting.

Michelle   Miss! Miss! Please Miss!

Celia   Yes, Michelle?

Michelle   Can I go toilet, Miss?

Celia   It's nearly the end of the day, Michelle. Can't you wait?

Michelle   No, Miss!

Celia   I'm sure you can.

Michelle   Can't, Miss!

Shane   'Course you can, you daft girl. Just shut your legs and suck.

Celia   Shane! That's enough! Where do you get such language from?

Shane   My dad.

Celia   I'm sure you don't, Shane.

Michelle   Miss! Miss!

Celia   Off you go, Michelle. But if I find you've decorated the corridor with toilet paper again, there'll be trouble.
               (Michelle exits.)

Justine   Please, Miss.

Celia   No, Justine, you can't go to the toilet. You've been three times already this afternoon.

Shane   Needs her washer fixed, don't she?

Celia   Shane! I won't tell you again! *(Pause.)* Right, then, I'll save my announcement until Michelle gets back. What shall we do in the meantime? I know, let's have a look at the lovely collages you've been working on this afternoon. *(She picks up a collage.)* Now, whose is this?

Jessica   That'th mine, Mith.

Celia   Oh, yes, I might have known. Ballet dancers.

Jessica   That'th my danthing clath at the Marthia Graveth Thtage Thcool, Mith Whibley. That'th me, doing a beautiful Arabethque, in the middle.

Celia	Oh, I see. How lovely!
Jessica	Can I do one now?
Celia	Do one what, Jessica?
Jessica	A Arabethque, Mith. I do beautiful Arabethqueth, Mith. Mith Bottomley, she told me my Arabethque wath the betht.
Celia	Would everyone like to see Jessica's Arabethque... I'm sorry, Arabesque?
Shane	I'd rather see her...
Celia	Shane! *(Without further bidding, Jessica does an ostentatious Arabesque in the middle of the class. Clapping enthusiastically.)* Oh, well done!
Shane	Was that it?
Jessica	That'th an Arabethque. *(She points to the collage.)* And that'th Amy, doing a awful entrechat, and that'th Tham, doing thloppy thecondth. Mith Bottomley only hath them in the clath to make money; she thayth *I'm* the only one with thtar potenthul.
Shane	Miss, why does Jessica talk funny?
Jessica	I hate you, Shane! You're thuch a pig!
Celia	Let's go on to the next collage, shall we? Oh, this one's... um... who did this one?
Dougal	That's mine, Miss Whibley. It's The Clifton Suspension Bridge. It was built by Isambard Kingdom Brunel who was one of the greatest of the Victorian Builders. He did not only make bridges. He also built the S.S. Great Britain, the first screw prop iron ship, and Temple Meads Station in Bristol.
Celia	Thank you, Dougal. Look, everyone, isn't this a good collage? And, oh, look, here in the corner, there's a little chuffer train.
Dougal	A slight anachronism, I'm afraid. I was interested to depict DNA (that's deoxyribonucleic acid, Miss) but I was unsure how to represent a double helix using a two-dimensional medium. However, the Clifton Suspension Bridge has a fine symmetrical form which is equally pleasant to the eye.
Celia	Yes? Never mind, Dougal. Well done. *(She turns to another collage.)* Oh, and what's this? There's an awful lot of red on this one.
Shane	Blood, Miss.
Celia	This is your collage, Shane? Your picture is very lively but I'm not sure what it is.
Shane	*(jumping up)*. It's *Terminator 3*, Miss. I know they haven't

made it yet, Miss, but I think it would be great, Miss. In this picture, Miss, Arnold Schwarzenegger is taking out the Terminator, but the Terminator can't be taken out, Miss, because they are indestructible, Miss. So the Terminator is killing all the police with his lazor Uzzi nine millimetre, Miss. Then Arnold Schwarzenegger throws some smart bombs but he kills some police and people at the shops by mistake. Look Miss, that's Sainsbury's. I think it would be great Miss, and I think that's better than boring ballet, Miss.

Celia   That's... um... very vivid, Shane. Very — imaginative.

Shane   It's great, Miss!

(Shane acts out the bloody attack, with Jessica (of course) as his principal victim. Much screaming and ad-lib dialogue. Celia steps forward to part the combatants and does so, after a struggle.)

Celia   Settle down now, 3C! That's really enough! *(Michelle returns and sits down. The class settles.)* Right then, where were we?

Shane   *(leaping up).* I was showing you my fighting, Miss.

Celia   *(firmly). Sit! (Shane looks a bit shocked and sits down.)* I was going to tell you all the good news, wasn't I? Well, it's this. Class 3C — it's our turn to do the Nativity play this Christmas. *(The reactions are varied.)* Now, I want you all to be in it. We need a Mary —

Shane   Can I play a Terminator Miss?

Celia   There are no Terminators in the Nativity, Shane. It is the story of the baby Jesus.

Jessica   Can I play Mary?

Celia   No, Jessica, I'm not going to choose the parts today. You'll all have to wait until tomorrow. What I would like you all to do is think about which part you'd like to play and who you think would be good in the other parts, too. Can you do that for me? *(The school bell rings. The children leap up.)* Goodbye then, 3C! See you all tomorrow!

(Ad-libbing goodbyes, the children leave. The Lights cross-fade to:)

Scene 3

A dining-room. There is a dining table C. Shane arrives home. Bob meets him.

Bob	Hallo, Shane, how's you? *(He gives Shane a big hug.)*
Shane	All right, Dad.
Bob	How was school?
Shane	Boring, Dad.
Bob	You always say that. Go on, tell me what happened.
Shane	What's for dinner, Dad?
Bob	Guess.
Shane	Fish fingers.
Bob	How did you know?
Shane	Tuesday, Dad.
Bob	Oh, right. Give me a hand setting the table, eh?
Shane	All right.
Bob	Forks go where?
Shane	In yer mouth, Dad.
Bob	Where do they go on the table, Shane?
Shane	On the top, Dad.
Bob	Funny man.
Shane	On the left, Dad.
Bob	Right. Forks on the left. *(They set the table during the following.)* I haven't been out all day, Shane, it's been really borin'. Ted Haskins was supposed to call me from the depot about some temporary job — but guess what? He didn't. And there wasn't a decent programme on the telly.
Shane	Boring.
Bob	Too right, Cheryl.
Shane	Who?
Bob	Sorry, mate. Forgot for a moment.
Shane	When is Mum coming back, Dad?
Bob	I don't think she is, Shane. Sorry.
Shane	Never? Never ever?
Bob	Never ever. It's not your fault, Shane, it's mine. She still loves *you*.
Shane	Yeah.
Bob	Spoons are pointing the wrong way, Shane.
Shane	Don't care.
Bob	Go on, you must have done something a bit different at

	school today — you're always doing different things.
Shane	Spencer Berryman honked up in dinner.
Bob	Oh, charming.
Shane	Red bits, Dad. All over his chair.
Bob	Thanks Shane, lovely.
Shane	Oh, yeah, Dad, and my class is doing the Nativity play.
Bob	The what?
Shane	You know, Dad, baby Jesus an' that. We're doing a play about it — in front of the whole school.
Bob	You gonna be in it?
Shane	Course I am. I'm goin' to be 'Erod the Great. He 'ad this huge sword and he slaughtered millions of babies and he tossed 'em up in the air and caught 'em on his sword or chopped 'em in 'alf or cut their heads off. I wanna be 'im. I'll make a 'uge sword and I'll show 'em.
Bob	Why'd he kill all those kids, then?
Shane	'Cause he didn't like 'em, I suppose.
Bob	Good job he's not around now — I wouldn't have you. *(Pause.)*
Shane	Don't be daft, Dad. Anyway, you'd have a big sword and you'd kill him. *(Pause.)* Wouldn't you?
	(Bob and Shane leave. Spencer enters and sits alone at the dinner table. His Mum and Dad are off in the shadows.)
Spencer	*(to us).* Spencer Berryman, who you didn't see in the classroom because he was lying in Matron's room with sick on his shoes, is eating his tea.
S's Dad	Eat it up, Spencer.
Spencer	Yes, Dad.
S's Dad	What's for our tea, love?
S's Mum	Same as Spencer, dear.
S's Dad	Oh, great.
S's Mum	Tell Dad your news, Spencer.
S's Dad	What's that, then, eh, Spencer?
Spencer	Nothing.
S's Mum	Oh, go on, Spencer, tell your father.
Spencer	Nothing.
S's Mum	No, it's not nothing, dear, it's good news.
S's Dad	What is it?
S's Mum	I'm not going to tell you, it's Spencer's news.
S's Dad	Spencer? *(Spencer says nothing.)* Oh, for Pete's sake,

Spencer, what is it, I haven't got all day!
(Spencer says nothing.)

S's Mum He's going to be in the Nativity play, aren't you, Spencer?

S's Dad A play? Him? Don't be bloody daft! He can't say boo to a goose… You'll never get him up on stage in front of the whole school. Probably die of nerves, eh, Spencer?

S's Mum It might be good for him — get him out of his shell.

S's Dad Out of his mind, more like.

S's Mum They say acting can help kids develop their confidence.

S's Dad Oh, really? Confidence? Where's a little squirt like Spencer going to find confidence? Eh?

(A long pause.)

Spencer Can I get down now, please?
(Spencer exits. Jessica and Melindra come forward and clear the table, tap-dancing as they do so.)

Jessica *(to us).* Jessica's mother…

Melindra *(to us).* … Melindra, ex-actress, still gorgeous at… um… forty-seven…

Jessica *(to us).* … was…

Melindra *(to us).* … overjoyed!…

Jessica *(to us).* … to hear about the play.

Melindra This is a golden opportunity, Jessica. Of course you'll be playing Mary, won't you, which is good because Mary always wears blue and that'll show up your colouring in the photographs… Photographs! I must find your portfolio toute suite. I'll phone your agent this evening — he can come down with some casting directors from London, good heavens, you never know, you might get spotted. And I must dig out your CV, darling — that'll impress Miss Whibley if she needs any persuading. Two pantos with the Barbara Bottomley Babes and a Sammy Snail No-Tears Shampoo commercial —

Jessica/Melindra …shown three times on S4C!

Melindra — will impress the Lycra all-in-one bodystocking off the girl! Don't know why I'm worrying, though, Jessie darling — I think the part was written for you.

Jessica I hope tho, Mummy.

Melindra Only one thing — what's her track record as a director? I'll phone the headmistress and check out her credentials… I'm not putting the career of my talented little darling in the hands of a mere amateur. Oh, I love this, don't you, darling?

The thrill of the chase! Oh, the theatre! I love it so much! (*To us*) It is inaccurate to call Melindra an ex-actress... She might not, now, be paid for it but she sure as hell never stops acting!

(Jessica and Melindra recede. Dougal and his MOTHER sit at the table. Dougal is reading a book on Nuclear Physics while his MOTHER plays Snap — more or less with herself.)

D's Mum   Three and three! Snap! I win again. Didn't you see that one, Dougal?

Dougal   I wasn't really concentrating, Mother.

D's Mum   Well. We'll carry on. *(She carries on.)* Is that a snap, Dougal?

Dougal   Two and seven, Mother. I think not. Modern philosophers might be able to prove that, theoretically, they are equal, but empirically, and bearing in mind the rules of the game, I have to say that no, indeed, that does not constitute the coincidence of numbering usually denominated as a snap in these circumstances.

D's Mum   Your heart's not really in it, is it, Dougal? What's the the matter?

Dougal   Well, I'm worried about this Nativity play, Mother. The second commandment specifically forbids the creation of craven images of our Lord. If we are to interpret that injunction in such a way as to include Jesus, his parents and close acquaintances — as which the Wise Men and Shepherds could conceivably be delineated — we would, in representing these figures theatrically, be blaspheming grossly, and could be laying ourselves bare to the wrath of the Lord Himself. This is an appalling conundrum and gives rise to a desperate crisis of conscience. *(Pause.)* All the same, I'd really like to be a Wise Man, I think.

(The Lights cross-fade to:)

Scene 4

A spot on Celia in the classroom

Celia   *(to us).* Well, I can't say I've slept very well. I've been so worried about casting the play, especially since Jessica's mother phoned me at seven this morning to tell me how talented Jessica is and how she'd be a natural for the part of Mary. Though how a red-haired lisping seven-year old tapdancer is supposed to be a natural for the part of a saintly pregnant virgin two thousand years ago in Palestine beats me! *(The Lights come up on the classroom. The children are there. To the children.)* Well, now, 3C, it's time to decide who's going to be who in the play. Let's start with —

Jessica   Mary, Mith. Let'th thtart with Mary. I've got my CV with me, Mith, and my agent'th addreth and —

Celia   Good heavens!

Jessica   And I can danth, Mith. Look, firtht pothisition, thecond pothisition...

Celia   Right, Jessica's playing Mary.

Michelle/Justine Oh, Miss!

Celia   I'm sorry, Jessica's the ideal choice. *(To us.)* Only because I'd never hear the end of it I cast her as a donkey or a sheep. *(To the children.)* Michelle and Justine, I think you two can be Angels, would you like that?

Michelle/Justine Oh, all right.

Celia   Good. Now, you boys...

Shane   Please, Miss, I want to be 'Erod.

Celia   Well Shane, 'Erod — I mean, Herod — doesn't normally appear in the Nativity play.

Shane   But 'e's brilliant, Miss. 'E's got a huge sword and he goes all over the place killin' babies.

Jessica   That'th horrible, Mith!

Shane   Yeah, and the only way to stop him is to have pitta bread and lamb chops and a pint of bitter herbs for your tea, Miss. If you don't, he picks up yer baby and he throws it in the air and he catches it on his sword and all blood and stuff comes out and the baby dies, Miss.

Celia   We're not having a Herod in our play, Shane. In fact, we're not having any characters with swords at all. And we're certainly not enacting the Massacre of the Innocents. *(To us.)* Tempting though it might be.

Shane	Oh, Miss…
Celia	Do you think you would like to play Joseph, Shane?
Shane	No.
Celia	Why not? He's a nice, gentle man who —
Shane	He don't do nothin', Miss. He don't have a sword or a dagger or nothin'. He's really borin', he just stands about lookin' supportive, Miss.
Celia	Well, someone else can play Joseph. I know… Spencer. You're a nice, gentle-looking person. You can play Joseph.
Spencer	*(bursting into tears).* Please, Miss, I don't want to be Joseph. I don't want to be in the play at all, Miss. Please, Miss, I feel sick, Miss, I want to go home, Miss… *(He holds the front of his trousers.)* Please, Miss, please, Miss…
Celia	Oh, Spencer, don't get so upset. There's nothing to worry about. *(To us.)* A sense of evangelical fervour has seized Celia; she is determined to bring out the best in Spencer. *(To Spencer.)* No, dear, you can be Joseph. And there's nothing to worry about. *(Spencer turns away.)*
Michelle	Ur, Miss, Spencer's honking again.
Justine	Ur, Miss, look, Jelly Tots…
Celia	*(to us).* Luckily, Spencer Berryman is so well-versed in being sick in class that he manages to get to the sink in time. Normality resumes minutes later… *(To the children.)* Now, then, we need an Innkeeper.
Shane	Does he have a sword, Miss?
Celia	No, Shane, he doesn't. He looks after the inn.
Shane	What's a inn, Miss?
Celia	A pub. Do you know what a pub is?
Shane	Course I do, miss. Men go there to get pissed.
Celia	Shane! Language!
Shane	I'll be a good Innkeeper, Miss. I can speak like a Innkeeper.
Celia	Oh, really.
Shane	Ain't you got no homes to go to? What time d'you call this, then, eh? Mine's a pint, squire!
Celia	Oh, that's very…
Shane	Do your talking while you're walking, this is a pub, not a club…
Celia	Lovely! That's enough now. Shane is the Innkeeper.

Shane	Can I be like a bouncer, Miss? With a knuckleduster and a breezeblock an' that?
Celia	No! Right, now, let's choose some Wise Men. I know, let's have some girls for this as well as boys. Melanie and Siobhan, you can be Wise Men, I think.
Melanie	I want to play a girl, Miss.
Celia	There aren't any girl's parts left, Melanie.
Melanie	Bein' a Wise Man's really borin', Miss.
Celia	No it isn't. You get to bring gifts to the baby Jesus and ride on a camel.
Shane	I'll be the camel if Melanie's gonna ride it!
Celia	Shane! Behave! And we'll have a little boy Wise Man as well. Craig, you can do that.
Melanie/Siobhan	Not Craig, Miss!
Celia	Why not?
Melanie	'E's 'orrible, Miss.
Siobhan	'E's got spots, Miss.
Melanie	'E 'as yogurt with his dinner, Miss.
Celia	Craig can't help what he looks like, any more than you can… and lots of people like yogurt.
Siobhan	Tastes like sick, Miss.
Melanie	Ask Spencer Berryman.
Celia	No, it doesn't. Now, I've decided. Craig will be the third Wise Man. Melanie, your present to the baby Jesus will be gold, Siobhan, yours will be frankincense, and Craig, yours will be myrrh…
Craig	What's myrrh?
Celia	Well, it's… It's a sort of… Does anyone know? *(Silence.)* Well, it's something very nice that babies like to play with, I suppose. What's next then? Goodness me, Shepherds. Now, we can all make a sheep noise, can't we? *(There is a cacophony of baa-ing. Jessica does a shepherdess dance.)* Good. *(Shane begins to howl and run around.)* Shane! What are you doing? That's not a sheep noise!
Shane	I'm being a wolf, Miss, biting the sheep.
Celia	Well, there aren't any wolves in this play, either, so you can be a sheep like everyone else.
Shane	Oh, Miss… *(He sits down.)*
Celia	But we need some of you to be Shepherds, don't we? Dougal, I think you'd make a good Shepherd.

Dougal   Well, actually, Miss, I was rather hoping to be cast as a Wise Man, but the role of a Shepherd would, I feel, be perfectly acceptable. They are, after all, devoid of pedagogical learning but possessed of an instinctive communion with the forces of nature, a Pantheistic appreciation of spirituality perfectly in keeping with many of my views on the subject.

Celia   Oh. Good. Does that mean you'll play a Shepherd for us, Dougal?

Dougal   Yes, Miss, it would be a pleasure.

Celia   I'm so glad.

Shane   Time, gentlemen, please.

Celia   Thank you, Shane…

(Pandemonium breaks out. Melanie and Siobhan taunt Craig — "Myrrh,myrrh!"; Jessica practises dance positions and looking holy; Spencer cries; Michelle and Justine practice 'flying' as angels; Shane howls and runs around; Dougal stands perfectly still, miming a crook and looking enigmatic. All the children bar Dougal, run off, followed by Celia. Dougal is left alone. He notices he's alone after a moment and, dropping his usually serious demeanour, skips round the stage singing "Old MacDonald Had A Farm"… and exits. The Lights cross-fade to:)

Scene 5

A wide spot. Miss Cusp and Miss Belcher, both smoking, appear. Dry ice begins to flow around their feet as they glide forward demonically

Cusp   *(to us)*. Miss Cusp —

Belcher   *(to us)*. — and Miss Belcher —

Cusp   *(to us)*. — are friends.

Belcher   *(to us)*. At least to each other's face.

Cusp   *(to us)*. And they both hate —

Cusp/Belcher *(to us)*. — Celia Whibley.

Cusp   Darling!

Belcher   Darling!

Cusp   The most awful news Belchy, dearest.

Belcher   Mr Miller's deodorant has given up the ghost again?

Cusp   No!

Belcher   Mr Elginbrod hasn't smiled at you today?

Cusp   No!

Belcher	Not that trouble with your…?
Cusp	No! No! No! Honestly, darling, that cleared up almost instantly, you know it did, but you have to keep on mentioning it, don't you?
Belcher	That's because I care, dear.
Cusp	Oh, but of course.
Belcher	Of course. Come on, pet, give us the lowdown. What's today's tragedy?
Cusp	Not news, exactly, just a dark premonition.
Belcher	Not one of your dark premonitions, Cuspy?
Cusp	The very same. I'm convinced, just convinced, that that idiotic wretch Whibley is going to make a first class success of the Nativity play. She's so nice, so popular — she's bound to get everyone on her side and put our efforts into the shade.
Belcher	Fear not, Cuspy — there's no chance she'll outshine us.
Cusp	True. We've had scenery filched from the Beeb…
Belcher	Oh, yes, clever Barry. He really was a find, Cuspy dearest. Pity you were already married to Gideon.
Cusp	I don't let things like that stand in my way, as you well know.
Belcher	How true.
Cusp	And, yes, we had a script written by Hengist Spreadbury —
Belcher	— who's written more episodes of *EastEnders* than you've had corrective surgery…
Cusp	Lights by that lovely Roger from the National.
Belcher	Sound by Ellis at the RSC.
Cusp	Costumes! No expense spared on those!
Belcher	The best Nativity play money could buy!
Cusp	Pity about the acting, though. Still, I suppose we did have to use the kids.
Belcher	It is *for* them, so I'm told.
Cusp	Not that it harms them if we grab a bit of glory on the side.
Belcher	That's not all you grabbed on the side, though, is it?
Cusp	Cusp and Belcher — Theatrical Entrepreneurs!
Belcher	The team of teams!
Cusp	And about to be scuppered by the odious Miss Goodwill!
Belcher	Only one way out, dear. One way to make sure we stay top dogs in the Nativity league.
Cusp	And that is?
Belcher	Sabotage!

Cusp	You mean — wreck her scenery? Tear her costumes? Burn her script?
Belcher	No, dear, something far less detectable. All we have to do is make sure no-one else gives her a hand. She'll never manage alone, will she?
Cusp	How true!
Belcher	A few well-placed words in a few suitably-attached ears and she'll be deserted!
Cusp	Alone!
Belcher	Up the creek without a paddle!
Cusp	Up the lane without a compass!
Belcher	Out of the plane without a parachute!
Cusp	Over the hills and far away!
Belcher	It's perfect!
Cusp	Subtle!
Belcher	And evil!
Cusp	And completely brilliant!
Belcher	Let's start right now!
Cusp	Yes, let's! And… Oh look! Here she comes! Let's do a little tormenting, shall we?
Belcher	Righto. Nice faces.
	(Celia enters. Cusp and Belcher smile terrifyingly.)
Cusp	Celia, darling!
Belcher	How are you, my pet? Everything going swimmingly?
Cusp	Dear me, you're looking awfully stressed.
Belcher	Dreadful bags under those eyes.
Cusp	More like a full set of matching luggage, darling.
Belcher	Is everything all right?
Celia	Well, no, not really. I'm a bit worried about the Nativity play. There's so much to do, so little time to do it in, as they say.
Cusp	You'll be fine, darling, there's absolutely nothing to worry about. You don't have to go it alone, after all. People will be just dying to help you, I'm sure.
Belcher	All you have to do is ask.
Celia	Really? You don't think anyone will mind?
Cusp	Of course not. We're all one big happy team here, aren't we, Belchy?
Belcher	Too true.
Celia	Well, in that case… You've both done loads of Nativity plays before —

Cusp	And very successfully, I may tell you!
Belcher	Marvellous reviews every time!
Cusp	Honed to perfection and gleaming with professionalism.
Belcher	The Nativity plays to end all Nativity plays.
Celia	So could you see your way to helping me with this one — just a little bit?
Cusp	My dear, I'm so sorry. Far too busy with other things.
Belcher	Life's an absolute whirl, Celia. Not a window in my diary until well into next year.
Cusp	But we're sure the other members of staff will be just delighted to help, won't they, Belchy?
Belcher	Oh, of course. Sorry, Celia.
Celia	That's all right . Well... Um... Goodbye, then.
Cusp	Bye, darling!
Belcher	And the very best of luck to you.
	(Celia exits, dejected.)
Cusp	Right! Let's get to the others before she does!
Belcher	I've actually just thought of a wonderful twist to our delicious little scheme.
Cusp	Oh, really? I love twists! Twist away!
Belcher	Let's get a complete show ready — call up the set, the lights, the costumes, everything!
Cusp	Get those husbands of ours to pay, eh?
Belcher	But of course! Then, when Celia's life is completely in tatters and nothing's been done for the Nativity play because no-one will help her...
Cusp	I get it! We step in and save the day! Cusp and Belcher, Saviours of the Universe. Just in the nick of time! It's perfect! We get to ruin her life and vastly improve our own! We'll do it!
Belcher	Good-oh! Let's get at it!
	(They exit evilly. The Lights cross-fade to:)

Scene 6

The classroom. Celia stands C. Around her, the children are engaged in rehearsals. Jessica is singing a children's Christmas carol and practising a hideously twee dance routine to go with it. Shane is miming opening and closing a door. Craig, Melanie and Siobhan are rehearsing as Wise Men.

Shane	*(to an imaginary Joseph).* Wodger want? A crash for the night? You'll be lucky, mate, we ain't got none. So hard luck.
Celia	*(to Shane).* That's not right, is it, Shane? The line is, "I'm sorry, but the inn is full. You may sleep in the stable if you wish."
Shane	*(in a ludicrously posh voice).* I'm sorry, but the inn is full. You may sleep in the stable if you wish.
Celia	That's better. *(She walks away.)*
Shane	Bog off, sunshine, there's no rooms here. Or you can kip down in the stable if yer must. Bleedin' scroungers! *Craig, Melanie, Siobhan.*
Craig/Mel/Siobhan	Look in the sky; it is a message from the Great God Almighty.
Melanie	What can it mean?
Craig/Siobhan	Shall we follow the star?
Craig	That's my line.
Melanie	No, it isn't.
Craig	Yes, it is.
Siobhan	You don't get to say anything by yourself. We're saying your lines now.
Craig	Why?
Melanie	'Cause you're a boy.
Siobhan	And you're spotty.
Melanie	And you eat yogurt.
Siobhan/Melanie	Yogurt — urr!
Craig	So what do I do?
Melanie	You stand behind us and keep quiet.
Siobhan	And when we get to the baby Jesus you give him the myrrh.
Melanie	But you don't say *nothing*!
Siobhan	Just hand over the myrrh and shut it. All right?
Melanie	All right?
Craig	All right. But what is myrrh?
Celia	*(approaches Spencer.)* Hello, Spencer. How are you getting

	on?
Spencer	All right, Miss.
Celia	Jessica, come over here a moment, please.
Jessica	Pleath, Mith, I haven't finithed my danth.
Celia	Never mind. Come over here and help Spencer with his lines.
Jessica	I'm good with lineth, Mith. I had to thay "Thammy Thnail No-Tearth Thampoo Keepth Your Hair All Thiny New", Mith, and it only took one take, Mith. The director thaid I wath wonderful, Mith.
Celia	Right. Now, what's your first line in the scene with Spencer?
Jessica	Jotheph, Jotheph, I am with child. *(Jessica and Celia look to Spencer for a response. There is none.)* An Angel of the Lord came down and did give me a baby, Jotheph.
Celia	Spencer hasn't said his first line, yet, Jessica. Spencer, what's your line?
Spencer	Don't know, Miss.
Celia	Yes, you do. You said it beautifully this morning when I was coaxing you out of the paint cupboard. Go on, say it for Jessica.
Spencer	Can't Miss.
Celia	Go on. "Dear Mary, I am overjoyed…"
Spencer	Can't.
Celia	Oh, please…
Jessica	Oh, Spenther, you're *tho* unprofethional, you'd be fired from the thet if thith were *real!*
	(Spencer bursts into tears.)
Dougal	*(as a Shepherd).* And, behold, above in the ether, what do I see but a star of an unusual aspect, most fiery and most beauteous, its gleaming rays signifying some special quality unbeknown to mortal man but pregnant with the mystery of the Deity…
Celia	Well, now, let's all rehearse together. We'll start with the Shepherds and the sheep…
	(Instant pandemonium; all the children become extremely loud and boisterous sheep. As the class reaches a peak, Mr MILLER bursts in.)
Mr Miller	*Silence!*
	(The children freeze and are silent.)
Celia	Mr Miller! *(To us.)* Old-fashioned disciplinarian and terrorizer of children and junior staff alike!

Mr Miller	Discipline, Miss Whibley, is what these children need. This boisterous behaviour will do them no good — nor the school. Do try, in future, to curb the excesses of their loutishness, Miss Whibley.
Celia	But they were rehearsing for their Nativity play.
Mr Miller	As you well know, I don't approve of plays. These children should be doing extra mathematics and woodwork, not plays.
Celia	Mr Miller, children need to exercise their imaginations…
Mr Miller	Nonsense! These children have too much imagination already! Discipline — that's what they need! *(To the class.)* Now, don't let me hear anything out of you lot again, or there'll be trouble! *(To Celia.)* Hard but fair, that's me, Miss Whibley, hard but fair. *(He goes.)*
Celia	Right, then, children. Let's try that again. Shepherds and sheep!
(The ch	*ildren move slowly round the room baa-ing very timidly and not enjoying themselves at all. The Lights slowly fade to black-out.)*

Scene 7

A spot comes up on Miss Cusp, C, talking on a mobile phone.

Cusp	As much crêpe de chine as you can lay your pinkies on, Monica… Blue of course, dear. We may be breaking records for taste and splendour for this production but Mary has always been in blue and we're not the types to fly in the face of convention… Oh, really? Well, all right, Monica, you can splash some heavenly gold on it. After all, if it's good enough for Liza Minelli… How is Liza by the way? *(Miss Belcher enters.)*
Belcher	Hello Cuspy. How's it going?
Cusp	I'm just talking to Monica at the costume place. It's all going to be just fine.
Belcher	For us anyway. *(They cackle evilly. The Lights cross-fade to:)*

Scene 8

The playground. The children are playing

Voice Over And when he came into the city the people brought forward their children so they could touch Him. But those that were with Him made to send the children away. He said to His followers, "Suffer little children to come unto me. For blessed is the person who comes unto me with the mind of the child."

(Jessica is reading her Nativity play script and looking very confused. She goes up to Shane who is sitting playing on the floor. She looks as if she is about to speak, then leaves him. She does this again. She looks at him. She smiles and goes away. She does this again.)

Jessica Thane?

Shane What do you want?

Jessica There'th something I don't underthtand.

Shane There are loads of things you don't "underthtand".

Jessica No, in the play. In the play I get my baby from God. But Mummy thaid that I come from both her and Daddy which ith a bit of a problem. Becauthe how did God give me the baby?

Shane Don't you know?

Jessica Know what?

Shane Where babies come from.

Jessica Yeth I do.

Shane Where then?

Jessica They come from… Well, the mummy and daddy have a baby and…

Shane You don't know do you?

Jessica Yeth I do.

(Justine and Michelle have been overhearing the conversation as they do.)

Justine *(asking knowingly).* What are you talking about?

Jessica Nothing. Go away.

Shane We're talking about where babies come from. And she doesn't know where they come from.

Jessica I do.

Michelle So where do they come from?

Shane Don't you know?

Justine We know. We wanted to know if you know.

Shane	I do.
Justine	No, you don't.
Michelle	Tell us, then.
Jessica	Go on, Thane. You think you're tho clever and you know everything.
Shane	Well, a man and a girl love each other and they kiss in a bedroom and later the girl goes to hospital all fat and comes out all thin and they have a baby which has been in the girl's belly. There I said I know.
	(The girls all stare at him. They look confused.)
Justine	Does that mean that in the play you have to go into a bedroom and kiss Spencer Berryman?
Jessica	I hope not.
Michelle	I'm glad that I'm an Angel, aren't you, Jus?
Justine	Yeah. You'll have to be careful, Jessica.
Jessica	Why'th that?
Justine	You know what Spencer Berryman's like, he might honk on you.
	(All the children laugh — except Jessica.)
Jessica	He won't, will he? That'th not very nithe. I don'th feel very well now. Thtop laughing at me.
Shane	You'll be covered in 'onk.
	(Enter Dougal.)
Dougal	Excuse me interrupting this childlike hilarity but the explanation of the origin of a baby given by Shane was somewhat simplistic.
Shane	No, it wasn't.
Dougal	Do be quiet, Shane. Shouting at me is no form of argument.
Jessica	Does that mean that I won't have to kith Thpenther Berryman?
Dougal	Well, let me explain. A male and the female of the species —
Justine	A what?
Michelle	A boy and a girl.
Justine	Why didn't he just say that?
Dougal	— are brought together by various means of attraction to become a mating couple.
Shane	Like friends.
Dougal	I'm sorry I didn't understand that last comment.
Shane	Mates. You know, friends.

Dougal	If you interrupt me I shall not continue.
Justine	Get on with it.
Dougal	Right, so insemination has to take place... *(The Lights fade rapidly, then come up again. All the children look shocked except for Shane, who is smirking.)* Once the egg has been fertilized it stays in the womb for a period of nine months... *(The Lights fade rapidly, then come up again. The girls look even more shocked. Shane has his hands up his jumper. He is hit by Justine.)* This is known as a contraction. When this happens the baby is ready to be born... *(Again the Lights fade down, then up. Shane is rolling around the floor laughing. All the girls look ill.)* ...and in certain societies this is eaten.
Jessica	I think I'm going to be thick.
	(Jessica exits at speed.)
Michelle	So she's going to do all that to Spencer Berryman?
Dougal	Don't be stupid. The play is representational.
Justine	So she won't have to do all that?
Dougal	Of course not.
Shane	Are you going to tell her?
Justine	No. Are you?
Shane	No.
Voice Over	Suffer little children to come unto me. For blessed is the person who comes unto me with the mind of the child.

(The Lights cross-fade to:)

Scene 9

The staff room. Miss Cusp, Miss Belcher, Kurt and Mr MILLER are all present. Octavia makes a grand entrance

Octavia	Good morning, team!
ALL	Good morning, Octavia!
Octavia	Celia Whibley is safely locked away, so to speak — she's having a rehearsal — so we can all discuss her progress without fear of embarrassing interruptions. Now, I hope she's receiving all the help she needs from her friends... *(Everyone tries to start a sentence but fails; they are all very twitchy and embarrassed. They eventually subside into silence.)* You're all just being modest, aren't you? I like that, you know, modesty — not blowing your own trumpet. Well

done, team. But just let your finer feelings off the hook for a moment and tell me. Let's start with you, Mr Elginbrod.

Kurt   Hey, Octavia, none of that surname stuff. A surname is just an emblem of patriarchal possessiveness and oppression. Please call me Kurt on all occasions; that's the name which expresses most fully my sense of spiritual independence and freedom from the trappings of culture and history.

Octavia   Very well... Kurt. I do hope you're giving Celia the help she requires; your skills as a musician, I've no doubt, will be of great benefit to her.

Kurt   Hey, Octavia! There's no way I can support the Nativity play; for a start, many other belief systems are represented in this school and we don't put on plays about them, do we?

Octavia   Well, you have a point there, Kurt...

Kurt   And what about humanism or existentialism, Octavia?

Octavia   For seven-year-olds?

Kurt   No problem, Octavia. I was quoting Jean-Paul Sartre at the age of seven...

Cusp   And look what good it did you!

Kurt   Hey, don't mock my personality. Our individualism is our gift, our particular right; mockery dents the aura, wounds the personality, taints the psychic pattern with negativity...

Octavia   The long and the short of all this is that you won't help with the Nativity play. Not one of your oft-conflicting, contradictory and half-understood philosophies —

Kurt   I'm closing my ears to this abuse!

Octavia   — can persuade you to give a little help?

Kurt   Don't oppress me! I won't be oppressed by the establishment.

Octavia   Don't worry, dear, the establishment's got better things to do. Mr Miller, I trust your contribution to Celia's efforts has been to your usual standard?

Mr Miller   Don't know why we have to do the same damn' fool play every year. Tell 'em to go to church, that's what church is for; teach 'em to be meek and mild and pay attention to their elders and betters, so we can just fill 'em up with knowledge. None of this imagination hoo-hah, this play-putting-on rubbish. Maths! Woodwork! Chemistry! Physics! Make real useful people out of them, workers and winners, not namby-pamby artists and actors and singers...

Octavia   You enjoyed doing the play last year, Mr Miller.

Mr Miller   So why wasn't I asked again, eh? Eh?

Octavia	Well, replacing the carols with spelling tests and multiplication questions did seem a little… Um…
Mr Miller	Hard but fair, Mrs Dutton-Griggs! Hard but fair!
Octavia	Quite. *(To Miss Cusp and Miss Belcher.)* And what about you, ladies?
Cusp	Well, we've had quite a long chat about this, haven't we, darling?
Belcher	Yes, we have.
Cusp	And we rather think that this is a perfect time to test Celia a bit. Hold back from offering help, keep in the background, and see how she gets on.
Belcher	It's amazing what people can achieve when they're left alone to struggle against the odds.
Cusp	True creativity!
Belcher	Personal development on a huge scale!
Cusp	A life-affirming battle against the old, scared self, leading to —
Belcher	Triumph!
Cusp	Insight!
Belcher	And spiritual completeness!
Octavia	My dears, you and I speak the same language!
Cusp	*(to us).* Funny, that!
Belcher	*(to us).* We'd been rehearsing that for weeks!
Octavia	And of course, you're absolutely right. Well done! Oh, dear Celia, the coming days will be a struggle, but you'll pull through, alone and powerful! Yes! It's perfect! The personal development opportunity of all time!
Kurt	Can we split, now, comrades? I have a crystal healing session with my class in five minutes.
Octavia	Yes, run along, all of you, chop chop. And thank you, girls, for your insight and care.
Belcher/Cusp	Thank *you*, Octavia!
	(Belcher and Cusp give each other a big thumbs-up. Everyone exits. Black-out.)

Scene 10

A wide spot comes up. Celia hurries across the stage. Octavia swoops down on her.

Octavia   Celia! How good to see you!

Celia   Good afternoon… Um… Octavia.

Octavia   Everything going well?

Celia   Well, actually —

Octavia   Good! Good! Celia, I am so proud of you. Going it alone with the Nativity play, refusing all offers of help in order to find your true self as an organizer, enabler and leader of men! Well done! (*To us*) Octavia Dutton-Griggs is adept, as many people are, at distorting the facts to her own ends. As Octavia's ends are generally positive, she thinks a little bit of a white lie now and then doesn'th hurt.

Celia   *(to us).* Except that Celia, who was about to ask for help with the set, the costumes, the music and the lighting for the play, can't do so now, as she doesn't want the headmistress to think she can't cope. So she just says *(To Octavia.)* Thank you. I do enjoy a challenge.

Octavia   Of course you do.

                   (Octavia leaves, beaming. Celia looks terrified and bereft.)

Scene 11

Celia   *(to us).* As Celia walks back to her class she thinks to herself I shall not let the actions of the other members of staff get to me. I can stand alone. But how? I don't feel very well. I now know why Spencer Berryman is always sick. I could have been a solicitor, a doctor, anything. Why me? *(The Lights come up on the classroom. The children are there.To the class.)* Right, class, I have some interesting news for you all. I think that it would be a good idea if we made our Nativity a little more special. Obviously I can't make all the costumes myself, so I think it would be a good idea if you all ask your mums and dads, or guardians, or foster parents, or children's home staff, or grandparents, or whoever to help out. Do any of you have any idea what you should wear?

Michelle   I think that the Angels should wear white and have big wings and an hallo.

Celia   I think you mean a halo, Michelle.

Michelle   Yes a hallo.

Celia   The word is halo.

Michelle	That's what I said, Miss.
Celia	Right. Does anyone else have any ideas? Jessica, I think that Mary should wear white, too.
Jessica	I think that Mary thould wear blue.
Celia	Why is that, Jessica?
Jessica	My mother told me, Mith. It would thuit my colouring, she said. She thaid I should have a blue dreth with a thort thkirt tho my legth will be free to tap danth.
Celia	But there isn't going to be a tap dance, Jessica. Mary doesn't tap dance.
Jessica	What doeth she do to entertain, then, Mith? Ith she a thinger? I can thing. Or doeth…?
Celia	She doesn't entertain, Jessica. She just gives birth.
Jessica	You mean, Mary'th not in show buthineth?
Celia	That's right, she isn't.
Jessica	Oh.
Celia	That's that settled, then.
Jessica	I can do ballet, Mith.
Celia	No ballet! No tap! No singing! Not even a comic recitation with fire-eating and juggling! Mary is Mary the Mother of God, she is not a contestant on *Stars in Their Eyes*, all right?
Jessica	Yeth, Mith.
Celia	What about the Shepherds?
Dougal	I take it it will be the traditional costume requirement?
Celia	It will.
Dougal	Then traditional it will be.
Celia	OK. The three Wise Persons, have you any ideas?
Melanie	We could wear football shirts.
Celia	Why would you want to do that?
Siobhan	Because of the song. "We three kings of Orient are".
Dougal	That's *the* Orient, not Leyton Orient.
Melanie	Well, how were we to know?
Celia	I think that your costumes should represent the gifts that you bring. I think that's the best information I can give you.
Craig	Miss, what is myrrh?
Celia	Right, I want you to tell your parents who you are if you haven't already and we'll see what you've come up with tomorrow. Right, what I want you to do is start with the beginning of the Shepherds. *(At this point all the children start to act like sheep. Chaos time. Lights down. Celia talks*

to us in a spot.) I've done it again. I've let them all be sheep. I do hope Mr Miller can't hear what is going on. *(To the children.)* Can you be a little more controlled about this? *(To us.)* I've got it! Thinking of Mr Miller has given me an idea of how to deal with the class. I have to be stern. No more mild-mannered Celia . Celia from Hell. And not just Celia the teacher but Celia the theatrical director. This show will be a success. This show will be a success. I'll show them. *(The Lights come up.)* Will you all be quiet? *(No response.)* I said, will you all be quiet? *(Shouting.)* Right you lot, hands on heads. *(All the children stop what they are doing and look at her, except Shane.)* And that means you too, Shane. *(Shouting.)* Shane! *(He stops in his tracks. Confused, he puts his hands on his head.)* Right you lot. There's not much time to make this show the best this school has ever seen. I'm going to rehearse and rehearse...

Melanie	Miss, what does rehearse mean?
Celia	Rehearse means doing it over and over again until it is right. And that is what we are going to do. We are going to do it over and over again until it is right. Are you all with me, kids?
Children	*(weakly).* Yes.
Celia	I'm sorry, I didn't hear that. Are you with me?
Children	*(shouting).* Yes.
Celia	OK, let's do it. Mary and Joseph, come out here to the front. We are going to start from the point where Mary has to tell Joseph that she has been visited by the Angel Gabriel. Right, off you go, Mary. *(Nothing happens.)* Jessica?
Jessica	Yeth mith?
Celia	Mary, that's you.
Jessica	Yeth Mith. *(To Spencer BERRYMAN.)* Jotheph, Jotheph, I have been visited in a dream and I have been chothen to be the mother of the thaviour of mankind. *(Spencer does not reply. He just looks worried.)* ... and I have been chothen to be the mother of the thaviour of mankind.
	(He still doesn't move.) Well? *(Still no reaction.)* What are you going to thay about that, Jotheph? *(Spencer just bursts into tears.)* Mith, Thpenther doesn't know his lines.
Spencer	I need to go to the toilet.
	(Spencer runs off.)
Jessica	Thpenther ith tho unproffethional.
	(Celia buries her head in her hands.)

Shane	*(standing to one side. To himself).* Heaven be praised. But Mary, my heart is heavy for we must travel to Bethlehem for the census.
Celia	Shane, what did you just say?
Shane	Nothin' Miss. I didn't say nothin'.
Jessica	He did, Mith.
Shane	Never.
Celia	Shane. For the first time in your life you didn't do something wrong. You know Joseph's lines.
Shane	I know all the words. I can remember things really easy.
Celia	Do you want to play Joseph? *(The Lights fade on the classroom, leaving Celia in a spot. To us.)* I actually said it. "Do you want to play Joseph?" I said. With all my problems I have just asked the loudest boy in the school to play the lead part in the Nativity play. I didn't think of the consequences, I just said it. And yet Spencer is so frightened and he does hold his thingy all the time and I'm sure that Joseph never held his thingy. *(The Lights come up.)* Well, what do you think?
Shane	What, me play Joseph with her?
Celia	It would help us out.
Shane	But Joseph doesn't do anything, Miss.
Celia	What do you mean he doesn't do anything?
Shane	He doesn't do anything. He doesn't own a pub or chuck people into the stable. He hasn't got a big sword or anything and all he does is go with Mary to Bethlehem and look all religious while lots of people visit Mary and the baby Jesus and that.
Celia	He's the most important character in the play, Shane.
Jessica	What about Mary, Mith? Mary'th the mother, she's really important.
Celia	Well, yes, but, Joseph has to protect Mary from —
Shane	Muggers, Miss. 'E duffs up the muggers in Bethlehem. 'E 'eadbutts 'em, puts the boot in, gives 'em a walloping…
Celia	I didn't quite mean protection of that sort, Shane…
Shane	'E'd 'ave to 'ave a knife, Miss.
Celia	No, Shane. No knives.
Shane	Oh, Miss.
Celia	Joseph is a man so powerful he doesn't need weapons, Shane. He's strong and proud and full of deathless conviction, so that people who see him fall back amazed

and say " Surely that man is the father of the Son of God?"

Shane	Really, Miss?
Celia	Really!
Shane	Oh, all right then, Miss. I'll play Joseph.
Celia	Oh, Shane, thank you!
Shane	As long as I can have a big stick.
Celia	Shane…
Shane	No stick, no Joseph, Miss.
Celia	All right! A stick! You can have a stick! You're Joseph!
Shane	But I'm not going to kiss Jessica.
Celia	You won't have to. And another thing Spencer Berryman will be pleased.
Shane	Do you think so, Miss?
Celia	I know so.
	(Spencer reappears.)
Spencer	*(to us).* And she is right. Spencer Berryman is delighted. *(He smiles at the audience. Black-out.)*

Scene 12

The lights come up on a darkened corner. Cusp and Belcher meet.

Cusp	It's going terribly well, darling. We're actually making the Whibley wobbly!
Belcher	You can stop that right now! It's cute, it's sweet, it's even vaguely affectionate.
Cusp	Right. No more jokes. Anyway, apparently she's so desperate she's asked the parents — the parents, I ask you! — to make the costumes.
Belcher	She's on the edge! She's ripe for a fall!
Cusp	And there's not a stick of scenery built.
Belcher	Any luck with Barry, by the way?
Cusp	Dinner at Espudo's and the possibility of diamonds, dear…
Belcher	Really?
Cusp	You know me, I'm good at making the best of my assets!
Belcher	So that's what you call them. *(Pause)* So, is he getting us some scenery?
Cusp	Darling, he's there. *(She indicates "under my thumb".)* He says we can have the pick of the Beeb's scenery. If we wanted to set the Nativity play on board a full-sized ocean liner, Barry would provide it.
Belcher	But we don't, do we dear?

Cusp	Oh, you can be so literal sometimes. I've put in an order and it'll arrive the day of the play... The more last-minute it seems, the more heroic we'll appear.
Belcher	Super.
Cusp	The Whibley might as well give up now and go back to Tesco's where she belongs. Oh, I do enjoy this — winning! *(Black-out.)*

Scene 13

The lights cross-fade to the dining-room. Shane arrives home. Bob arrives into the light.

Bob	Hallo, Shane. *(Gives Shane a big hug.)*
Shane	Dad, Dad, Dad...
Bob	Keep your hair on, Shane. What's so exciting, then?
Shane	Dad, Miss Whibley's asked me to play Joseph.
Bob	That's great, that is. Well done! Better than that old Innkeeper, innit? My son's goin' to be a star! Today, Verruca Street Church of England Primary School, tomorrow — Hollywood! *(He gives Shane another big hug.)* I'm proud of you, son.
Shane	Miss Whibley said you've got to make my costume, Dad.
Bob	What?
Shane	She ain't got time to make the costumes so all the mums and dads 'ave to do it.
Bob	Strewth, Shane, I can't make costumes. What does Joseph wear, then?
Shane	A little sort of dressing-gown thing and a cloth on his head.
Bob	Well, you've got a dressing-gown, aintcha? Use that.
Shane	It's got Mutant Ninja Turtles on it, Dad.
Bob	Wear it inside out.
Shane	Oh, Dad...
Bob	Sorry, son. I know this is important to you. We'll have to think of something really special. *(Spencer enters and stands C, looking upset and with his hand in his pocket. His parents are off in the shadows as before.)*
S's Dad	He's what?
S's Mum	He's been replaced as Joseph in the Nativity play, dear.
S's Dad	He's been what?
S's Mum	Replaced, dear.
S's Dad	Sacked, you mean! I told you he was no good for

	anything… the little pipsqueak!
S's Mum	He *is* going to play the Innkeeper, though, dear.
S's Dad	Oh, great! One moment a star, the next a glorified extra. My brilliant son. And I bet he didn't contest it, did he? No way… He wouldn't say boo to a goose! Spencer, why couldn't you do something I'd be proud of, just once? Why can't you be more like your brother?
S's Mum	Darren's in borstal, dear.
S's Dad	So! At least he had a go!

(Spencer pulls his hand out of his pocket. He holds a toy pistol. He points this at his father and smiles.)

Spencer	*(to us).* Boo!!

(Jessica arrives home. Melindra comes forward.)

Jessica	Hello, Mummy.
Melindra	Tough rehearsal, darling? Never mind — it'll be worth it in the end. Vanessa Redgrave said to me *(To us.)* and to a thousand others when she gave a lecture at the university *(To Jessica.)* "You must ride the storm, fight the good fight, and act as if your life depended on it." Oh, Vanessa, she's such a professional. Never made it as a Tiller Girl, mind you, but then we can't all be multi-talented, can we?
Jessica	Mummy, Mith Whibley thaid I can't do a danth in the play.
Melindra	Did she? Did she? We'll soon see about that.
Jessica	I think it'th jutht an acting part, Mummy.
Melindra	Acting, darling? But that's not what the public will be there to see. They want sparkle, music, romance, magic and a powerful central performance from a star dripping charisma — in this case, you!
Jessica	I'll do my betht, Mummy.
Melindra	Of course you will — because your best is my best, never forget that.
Jessica	Mith Whibley told uth to athk our mummieth to make our costumeth, becauth she doethn't have time.
Melindra	Excellent! Darling, I anticipated this, and I've been up to John Lewis and picked up as many swatches as I can. They've got lovely blues, dear, with some excellent co-ordinating bordering. It's ages since I've made a dress, but I'm sure I've not lost my touch. You'll look so beautiful the casting directors won't be able to resist you!

(Dougal arrives home.)

Dougal	I have given serious study recently to the subject of ancient Palestinian textiles. I am assuming that the Shepherds of

the Bible story would have reserved some of the wool from their sheep for their own use and would, therefore, be dressed in woollen goods rather than cotton or linen. On a loom designed to be as similar as possible to those used at the time (which information I gleaned from a specialist book on the subject ordered from the local library, a facility invaluable to the serious researcher) I have, using untreated wool collected from the barbed wire of the sheep fields next to my grandfather's house, woven a small piece of a rough woollen fabric that is, I believe, as close to the original as possible and which should, I believe, be used in the making of all the costumes in our play. *(Pause.)* It has to be said, however, that it took me three days to make a piece of extremely itchy cloth four inches square, so I suppose we'll have to make do with dressing-gowns and tea towels.

(Black-out.)

Scene 14

The lights come up on the classroom. The children are rehearsing.

Justine   We are Angels of the Lord and we have come unto Narareth to bring you tidings of great joy.

Michelle   You will be entered by the Holy Spirit and the great God will visit you in a shaft of light. And lo you shall have a child and it will be known as King of Kings.

Justine   And the heavens will be praised.

Michelle   Do you know what all this means?

(Justine shakes her head. Black-out. Lights up.)

Jessica   Jotheph, Jotheph, I have been visited in a dream and I have been chothen to be the mother of the thaviour of mankind.

Shane   Heaven be praised. But Mary, my heart is heavy for we must travel to Bethlehem for the census.

Jessica   Then off we shall go.

Jessica/Shane To Bethlehem.

Celia   That's very good, you two; keep it up.

(Jessica and Shane smile falsely at each other. Lights down. Lights up. Melanie and Siobhan speak together, Craig about half a second behind.)

Craig/Melanie/Siobhan Look in the sky; it is a message from the Great God Almighty.

Melanie   What can it mean?

Siobhan   Shall we follow the star?

Craig   That's my line.

Siobhan   No, it's not, it's Mel's, isn't it?

Melanie   Yes.

Craig   Well, you would say that, wouldn't you?
(Lights down. Lights up.)

Jessica   Are there any roomth in your lowly but comfortable-looking inn for I am weary and with child? *(Spencer doesn't answer.)* Well…
(Lights down. Lights up.)

Dougal   Roboam, Aminadab. Come here. Miss, notice how I have chosen authentic biblical names for my dogs.

Celia   Very good, Dougal.

Dougal   I anticipated such a response.
(Michelle and Justine fly around the stage in formation.)

Michelle   Fear not Shepherds, for we bring you glad tidings of great joy.

Justine   Yer.
(They flutter a little more.)

Dougal   Excuse me but I cannot escape from the perception that the movements you are making are considerably more reminiscent of bats than the angelic phenomena you wish to represent.

Justine   Well, no-one asked you.

Dougal   I was merely offering my opinion.

Michelle   Just say your words, brain box.

Dougal   Heavenly portent, what do you want with us?

Justine   You what?

Michelle   You must follow the star for the Saviour of Mankind is upon us.
(They sweep around the stage. They dive bomb the Shepherds and exit.)

Dougal   *(under his breath).* I would almost suggest the Dam Busters March as a theme but I would hate to trivialize the piece.
(Lights down. Lights up.)

Jessica   Pleathe thay thomething Thpenther.
(There is no response. Lights down. In the black-out…)

Craig   Will you stop picking on me.
(Lights up.)

Shane   Come on, Jess, let's do the bit where we're walking through Bethlehem and I'm protecting you. *(He grabs Jessica and leads her along. To Dougal.)* What choo lookin' at, then,

	eh? Want a bunch of fives up yer 'ooter?
Celia	Shane, what are you up to?
Shane	I'm protecting 'er, Miss. *(To Dougal.)* Lay a finger on my girl and I'll rip yer 'ead off, Shepherd-Brain!
Jessica	Thane, you're hurting me!
Celia	I think you'd better let go of Jessica, Shane. Protecting her is one thing, squeezing her to death is quite another. Now, let's see how the Angels are getting on…
Michelle	Humble Shepherds, this is the place where you shall pay homage to the king.
Dougal	O gracious heavenly host, thou be praised.
Justine	What?
	(The Angels flutter around. Dougal trips Michelle up.)
Michelle	Right, brain box, you're for it.
Justine	That's not in the script.
	(Lights down. The sound of fighting. Lights up.)
Jessica	Thpenther Berryman, you are hopeleth.
Celia	*(to us).* As much as it goes against my better judgement, I have to agree with her. Spencer Berryman is useless.
Jessica	*(to Spencer).* Are there any roomth in your lowly but comfortable-looking inn for I am weary and with child?
*(Spen	cer is silent.)*
Celia	Spencer…
Spencer	*(with a great effort).* I'm sorry…
	(He grinds to a halt.)
Celia	Yes, Spencer?
Spencer	*(after a huge and breathless pause).* I'm sorry, but the inn is full. You may sleep in the stable if you wish.
Celia	Oh, Spencer, well done! Well done! *(To us.)* Celia is ecstatic! Spencer has just said his line! A major break-through has just been made.
Shane	Miss, Craig has just hit the other two Wise Men.
Celia	*(shouting).* Persons. Right, I'm going to bang your heads together.
Shane	Can I do it?
Celia	You're welcome.
Jessica	Thith is a thambolth.
Shane	Miss, did you know the Angels are fighting with the Shepherds?
Celia	You hum it, I'll play it.
Shane	What?

Celia   The old jokes are the old jokes, Shane. *(Bell.)* Saved by the bell. That's it, everyone. Have a good evening. Don't do anything too dangerous. *(Manic laugh.)* Bye bye, T.T.F.N, bon soir, aufwiedersehen, toodle-oo, thank you and goodnight. *(The children exit.)* What can I do?
              (The Lights cross-fade to:)

Scene 15

The dark corner. Cusp and Belcher meet.

Belcher   Have you seen her? Mooning about the hall looking very sorry for herself.

Cusp   Poor pet! And is there any scenery on hand?

Belcher   Not a bit.

Cusp   Excellent! Lights?

Belcher   It's as dark in there as the bags under your eyes, dearest.

Cusp   Costumes?

Belcher   Not a stitch as yet.

Cusp   Better and better!

Belcher   She doesn't stand a chance, dear!

Cusp   Unless she can do miracles. She's got less than a day to get the entire show together... You're right, she doesn't stand a chance! And when she's on her knees, weeping for mercy, all we do is ring up Bosco...

Belcher   Bosco?

Cusp   Trust me, dear. Mate of Barry's. All I have to do is ring Bosco and three pantechnicons full of goodies will arrive, with hunky techies to put it all together — and our place in the annals of theatre history is assured!

Belcher   Wonderful!

Cusp   And just as an indulgence, I got on to Stax and Booter...

Belcher   Who?

Cusp   Motorcycle outriders, sweetie. Enough throbbing machinery and sweaty leather to keep a couple of swingers like us very happy.

Belcher   Think this calls for a drink!

Cusp   Too true, darling! The Bollinger's on me!
              (They exit victoriously. The Lights cross-fade to:)

Scene 16

The school hall. Evening. Celia sits in the middle of the room, looking depressed.

Celia   Right. One set coming up. Mary and Joseph's house, the road to Bethlehem, the exterior of the inn, the interior of the stable, the hills above Bethlehem … Oh, no that's not one set, that's five sets, and there's only one night to go and only me to do it. I might as well admit defeat right now … *(Pause. Bob enters.)*

Bob   'Ello, Miss Whibley, you all right?

Celia   You're Shane's dad, aren't you?

Bob   That's right, er … Miss …

Celia   Celia.

Bob   Right. And I'm Bob. You do realize it's half past eleven at night, don't you? I was driving past and thought you must be getting burgled! Didn't expect to find you here, all alone.

Celia   I'm supposed to be getting the set ready for tomorrow's performance, but there's so much to do and no-one has offered to help and I don't know where to start and … *(She cries.)*

Bob   'Ere, don't cry. I was a chippy until I was made redundant. I'll help you build the set. It'll be as easy as falling off a log. I can stay all night if you want, Shane's sleeping at his Nan's. I've a good idea why don't I ring some of the other parents and we'll see what we can do tonight? I'll use the phone in the office. *(He heads off.)* This will be the best Nativity the school has ever seen. *(Black-out.)*

Scene 17

The lights come up on Celia, Bob, Melindra and D's Mum.

Celia   Well, thank you all for rallying round at my time of need… Heavens, I sound like Octavia! What shall we do first? *(They all start to speak at once. Eventually Bob shouts them down.)*

Bob   'Ere! 'Ang on! This is no good! I reckon we start with the lights! *(He exits.)*

Celia   Do you know anything about lights, Bob? *(They are plunged into impenetrable gloom.)* No, you don't. Never mind, let's get on… *(During the following sequence, various inappropriate Lights* come up, illuminating short "snapshots" of action. Any prop jokes that seem appropriate should be inserted between the following. A Light comes up on D's Mum. She is enthusiastically painting a flat and singing "If I Ruled the World" in a wobbly Scottish contralto. Black-out.)

Bob   (off) Sorry!

              (Two follow-spots dance around the stage.)

Celia   Bob, you're doing the lights for a stage show, not manning the watchtower at Alcatraz!

Bob   (off). Sorry!

              (A Light comes up on D's Mum. She is sitting on a chair, still painting the same flat, and beginning to look tired. She is singing "Windmills of Your Mind" rather half-heartedly. All the Lights come up, extremely brightly. Melindra walks on, wearing sunglasses and carrying a toilet brush.)

Celia   (off). Where are you going with that toilet brush, Melindra?

Melindra Well, I just thought…

Celia   (off). This is the year nought A.D. Get rid of that brush!

Melindra It is wood-effect, Miss Whibley. John Lewis.

Celia   (off). No! No! No!

Melindra (barking). A lavatory without a brush is a potent symbol of the declining standards of hygiene in modern Britain and it breaks my heart! I have to take a toilet brush with me everywhere I go — I can't trust other people to meet my requirements. And I think you'll find the Virgin Mary felt the same!

              (Melindra storms off. Celia enters and looks up, as if to Bob.)

Celia   That's too much, Bob, sorry.

Bob   (off). You want less light?

Celia   Just a touch.

              (Black-out.)

Bob   (off). Sorry.

              (The Lights come up on D's Mum. She is sitting on the floor, painting extremely slowly, and singing " A Hard Day's Night". Celia approaches her.)

Celia   Four o'clock! Good heavens, doesn't time fly when you're having fun?

D's Mum   Yes, it does. It also goes quite pleasantly when you're at home in bed at four in the morning.

Melindra (moves C.) Now, Robert, a word to you about colours…

Bob	*(off).* Colours?
Melindra	In the lights, dear. It's vital that Jessica is lit throughout in pink — it really is the colour that makes her look her best. Can you find me a nice pink? *(Black-out.)*
Bob	*(off).* Don't think so. *(Several vile-coloured Lights come up, Melindra reacting to them with increasing horror. There is no pink.)*
Bob	*(off).* Sorry, that's it.
Melindra	No pink?
Bob	*(off).* No pink.
Melindra	Got anything puce-ish?
Bob	*(off).* Got yellow.
Melindra	No.
Bob	*(off).* Mauve.
Melindra	No.
Bob	*(off).* Ish.
Melindra	How ish? *(A ghastly purple comes up.)*
Melindra	*(defeated).* That's ish enough.
Bob	*(off).* Oh, what's this here? Good heavens, Light Red. Ish. *(A perfect pink Light comes up.)*
Melindra	Oh, Robert, you were teasing me. That's all the ish I shall ever need. *(Black-out.)*
Celia	*(from the gloom).* Six o'clock and everyone's still smiling! *(A Light comes up on D's Mum. She is lying flat on the floor, fast asleep, but with one hand still slowly painting the flat.)*
Bob	Right. Let's see what this does. *(There is a tremendous explosion, with smoke, then a black-out. Heavenly music. The Lights come up very slowly to reveal a complete set, gleaming and lovely. Standing in the midst of it are Cusp and Belcher, absolutely furious.)*
Cusp	She's done it. The bitch has done it! *(Enter Shane.)*
Shane	'Ere Miss, there's two blokes outside on dirty great big motorbikes. One's a Harley Davidson, Miss and the other's a Honda Goldwing. Dead sexy bikes, Miss.
Belcher	That'll be your motorcycle outriders, Cuspy. Seem a tad superfluous at this juncture. Were there any lorries with the bikes, Shane?

Shane	Yeah, miss, three 'uge ones. Mega. Ginormous. Humongous. And really big.
Cusp	All right, I get the picture!
Belcher	Monica…
Cusp	Barry…
Belcher	Bosco…
Cusp	Stax…
Belcher	Booter…
	(During the following, like two Wicked Witches of the West, Cusp and Belcher sink to the floor, screaming in frustrated agony.)
Cusp	The humiliation! The outrage!
Belcher	I can't stand it! I'll never be able to hold my head up in public again!
Cusp	I might as well sell my handbag collection and move to Wigan!
Belcher	Oh, God, why can't I get work in the private sector!
Shane	Shall I tell them to go away, Miss?
	(Black-out.)

Scene 18

Voice Over I am Alpha and Omega, the beginning and the end. The first and the last. Blessed are they that do His commandments, that they may have the right to the Tree of Life and may enter through the gates of the city of Heaven. *(The Lights come up on the school hall stage. Octavia comes to the front of the stage.)*

Octavia Ladies and gentlemen, mummies and daddies, guardians, foster parents, children's home staff, grandparents, or whoever; Reverend, staff and pupils. Welcome to Verruca Street Church of England Primary School's annual Nativity play. I hope that this year's performance will be a special one. A unique and moving portrayal of the birth of our Lord, Reverend. So strike up the band, let the show commence, because there is no business like show business. The first carol is *Silent Night.* That is number 5 on your song sheets. *(She exits. Bad piano playing. The children kill the first verse of "Silent Night". Celia, off stage, acts as Narrator.)*

Celia *(off).* For it was written that in Nazareth a virgin would be chosen. That virgin was visited by an Angel with tidings of great joy. *(Enter Justine, in a beautiful Angel costume.)*

Justine I am the angel of the Lord. I have come unto Bethlenehemn... Bethlenhem... Bethlehenmum... Bethlehem... n.

Celia *(off).* Nazareth dear. You're in Nazareth.

Justine Narazeth to bring you tidings of great joy. *(Enter Michelle, in an extremely tatty Angel costume.)*

Michelle You will be entered by God on a shaft of light and give birth to the low king of all kings.

Michelle/Justine Heaven be praised. *(They exit in formation. Enter Shane. He paces around. Enter Jessica.)*

Jessica Jotheph, Jotheph, I have been visited in a dream and I have been chothen to be the mother of the thaviour of mankind. They were tidings of great joy.

Shane Heaven be praised, great joy. But Mary, my heart is heavy for we must travel to Bethlehem for the census and to pay our council tax.

Jessica Then off we thall go.

Jessica/Shane To Bethlehem. *(A verse of "Little Donkey". Shane and Jessica march* *around the stage pretending to ride a donkey. Shane acts aggressivelyhe thinks of himself as an armed guard, ad-libbing being hard to members of the audience:" Are you looking at my bird?" etc.)*

Celia *(off)*. And Mary and Joseph travelled for — um — oh, forty days and forty nights, I suppose — until they arrived in Bethlehem. *(Shane is still shouting at the audience, protecting Mary Louder; off.)* And Mary and Joseph travelled for forty days and forty nights until they arrived in Bethlehem... *(Shane continues. Even louder; off.)* I said!... *(Shane continues. Entering, furious.)* Shane! Stop that this instant! *(To us.)* He's so high-spirited, you know. *(To Shane.)* Come on, Shane, I think Mary can cope quite well without you.

(Shane goes off, ashamed, with Celia.)

Jessica Oh. Here I am, all alone in Bethlehem. *(Pause.)* I know, I will do a danth to path the time.

Melindra *(off)*. That's my girl, Jessica! Sparkle! Remember, charisma!

(Jessica begins a hideous tap routine.)

Spencer *(off)*. No, Miss.

Celia *(off)*. Oh, Spencer, you have to go on; no-one else knows your line!

Shane *(off)*. I do, Miss.

Celia *(off)*. You're already playing Joseph, Shane. After a fashion.

Spencer *(off)*. I'm not going on, Miss.

Celia *(off)*. Yes, you are.

Spencer *(off)*. No, I'm not.

Celia *(off)*. Yes, you are.

Spencer *(off)*. I'm not, Miss.

Celia *(off)*. The hell you're not!

(Spencer appears, travelling at speed. The moment he sees the audience, he freezes.)

Jessica Oh, there you are, worthy innkeeper. Are there any roomth in your lowly but comfortable-looking inn for I am weary and with child? *(Silence.)* Are there any roomth in your lowly but comfortable-looking inn for I am weary and with child? *(Silence.)* Worthy Innkeeper, pleath thay thomething. *(Silence.)* Anything. *(Silence.)*

Celia *(off)*. Try again, Jessica.

Jessica Are there any roomth in your lowly but comfortable-looking inn for I am weary and with child? Thpenther? *(Silence.)* You thaid it before, Thpenther. I heard you.

(Spencer makes a huge effort to speak. It is no good. We hear Celia whispering offstage; then…)

Dougal *(off).* Are you sure, Miss?

Celia *(off).* It's the only way, Dougal.

(Dougal enters, with an apron tied round his dressing-gown Shepherd's outfit.)

Jessica Behold, who comes here?

Dougal Lo, for I, a passing Shepherd earning a few extra shekels manning the bar at this inn, have been sent here with a message from the Innkeeper's wife. There are no rooms available in this establishment at present but you are at liberty to avail yourselves of the stable for sleeping and maternity purposes, should you wish to do so.

Jessica Thank you. Let us depart. *(They head for the exit.)* Did you make all that up, Dougal?

Dougal Of course. The master of improvisation.

Jessica You're so clever, Dougal.

Dougal I know.

(They exit.)

Celia *(off).* Spencer, you can come off now. *(Spencer is rooted to the spot, holding the front of his trousers. Celia dashes on.)* Oh, don't do that with yourself, Spencer, it isn't nice.

Spencer Yes it is.

(Celia drags Spencer off. They all sing one verse of "We Three Kings". Enter Michelle as the star. She is unhappy.)

Michelle I am the star that shall shine down as a beacon to guide the faithful to our Lord.

(Enter the three Wise Persons. Melanie is dressed in gold. Siobhan is dressed as Frankenstein's Monster. Craig is in normal clothes and a turban. The Star sighs and looks bored.)

Craig/Melanie/Siobhan Look in the sky; it is a message from the Great God Almighty.

Melanie What can it mean?

Craig *(before Siobhan can say it).* Shall we follow the star?

Siobhan You're not supposed to say anything on your own.

(She hits him. Siobhan storms off, followed by Melanie and Michelle.)

Craig Miss, why is Siobhan dressed as Frankenstein?

Celia	*(off)*. I told her mother frankincense. What she heard is not my responsibility. Siobhan's supposed to be reflecting the gift she's bringing. Like you.
Craig	Miss, I didn't know what myrrh was, Miss.
Celia	*(off)*. What are you doing?
Craig	I don't know, Miss.
Celia	*(off)*. Well, get off stage, then.
Craig	Righty-o, Miss.
	(Craig exits.)
Celia	*(off)*. In the hills some humble Shepherds look over their flocks.
	(They sing "While Shepherds watch their flocks by night." Enter Dougal, with Michelle, Justine and Jessica as sheep.)
Dougal	My sheep are content. See how they gambol peacefully in the greensward. *(Sheep chaos; Shane enters and chases Michelle, Justine and Jessica.)* Robaom, Aminadab!
Celia	*(putting her head round the scenery)*. What's going on? *(She sees the chaos.)* Good heavens!
Dougal	If you would oblige me with some barking, Miss Whibley, we may well be able to get this scene back on an even keel.
Celia	Barking, Dougal?
Dougal	There's no-one else left, Miss. *(Celia barks loudly. The children instantly become good sheep.)* Perfect. Now we can proceed.
Celia	You're amazing, Dougal.
Dougal	An observation that's frequently made, Miss Whibley.
	(Celia vanishes back behind the scenery.)
Celia	*(off)*. And it came to pass that these certain Shepherds received a visitation from all the heavenly host… *(No Angels appear.)* And it came to pass… Oh, er, Angels? Could you stop being sheep please and become Angels again?
Michelle	'Ere, Justine?
Justine	Baa, baa… What?
Michelle	I think we're needed.
Justine	What?
Celia	*(off)*. And it came to pass that these certain Shepherds received a visitation from all the heavenly host… *Angels where are you?*
	(Michelle and Justine leap to their feet.)
Michelle	Behold, we bring you tidings of great joy. In Bethlehem a

	child is born and His name is called Emanuel…
Justine	I thought his name was Jesus.
Michelle	Jesus Emanuel, I guess.
Justine	But God's his dad. Shouldn't his name be Jesus Emanuel God, Miss?
Celia	*(off)*. Get on with it!
Dougal	My best endeavours shall be done therein. That's Shakespeare, so much better than the line in the script.
Celia	*(off)*. Oh, for goodness' sake. *Next scene! Next scene! Next scene !*
	(The sheep, angels and Shepherd rush off. Spencer enters at speed.)
Spencer	*(in one breath)*. I'm sorry, but the inn is full. You may sleep in the stable if you wish.
Celia	*(off)*. Oh, Spencer! *(Celia dashes on.)* You're a star, Spencer! You finally plucked up the courage to say your line! Well done! *(Celia gives Spencer a big hug. They exit. Off.)* In a stable in Bethlehem the Saviour of Mankind was born. For from this humble stable the King of Kings came into the world to deliver us all from evil.
	(Enter Shane and Jessica.)
Celia	*(off, whispering)*. You've forgotten the baby Jesus.
Jessica	What?
Celia	*(off)*. The baby Jesus.
Jessica	What about it?
	(Celia throws a doll on. Shane catches it by the leg and hands it to Jessica. She takes the baby and holds it to her breast.)
Shane	'Ere, you look like you're feeding it.
Jessica	No, I don't.
Shane	Good job you're not; you ain't got anything.
Celia	*(off)*. Get on with it, Shane.
Shane	It is a beautiful child, Mary.
Jessica	It ith because it ith the Thon of God.
Shane	*(under his breath)*. Flatty.
Jessica	I am not.
Shane	Are.
Jessica	Well, I am only theven.
	(Jessica storms off, dumping the baby on Shane. Enter the three Wise Men.)
Melanie	Oh, joy of joys. We have travelled from — er — somewhere

else to pay homage to the Son of Man.

Craig   We bring you Gifts from the east.

Melanie   Gold. A symbol of kinglyness.

Siobhan   Frankenstein. Symbol of wisdom and goodness.

Craig   And myrrh. A symbol.

Siobhan   Take these gifts, holy one. Praises be to the King.

(They exit backwards bowing, causing havoc. Re-enter Jessica.)

Jessica   Jotheph, I have forgiven you. I know it ith wrong for the mother of the Thon of God to argue with the father of the Thon of God.

Shane   I'm not the father of the Son of God. God is the father of the Son of God.

Jessica   Doeth that mean that you have forgiven me?

Shane   Yes, as long as I don't have to kiss you. But look here come the Shepherds.

(Enter Dougal; all the others come on as sheep.)

Dougal   Greetings, Mother and Foster-father of the King of All Creation. I bring you glad tidings of joy from the wool and mutton trades, and all associated industries in the area of meat and textile production. As a gift, I am pleased to present you with this very charming and beautiful sheep *(He drags one forward.)* which I hope you will accept with our good wishes.

Shane   Stick to the script, Dougal, I wanna get home in time for *Power Rangers*.

Dougal   Very well. Lo, I bring a gift of a fine sheep to bless the new-born King.

Shane   Amen, amen, I say to that, and glory be to God. For you, Shepherd, with your simplicity, exemplify the message of this Nativity.

(Tableau. Then the children bow and exit. Octavia enters.)

Octavia   Ladies and Gentlemen, mummies and daddies, guardians, foster parents, children's home staff, grandparents, or whoever; Reverend, staff and pupils. I'm sure you'll all agree with me when I say that this has been one of the most... um... the most... one of the most... plays we've ever had at Verruca Street Church of England Primary School. And we have but one person to thank for this — Celia Whibley!

(Celia enters shyly, being led by Shane and Jessica; the other children group round her.)

Celia	Thank you, thank you, oh, yes, thank you everyone! *(The children line up and start to sing "We Wish You A Merry Christmas" quietly under the following dialogue.)*
Octavia	Yes, my dear, it really was a sterling effort, possibly the best ever…
Celia	Well, that's very nice of you, Octavia, but, surely, it was a dreadful mess; children misbehaving, forgetting their lines, getting everything wrong…
Octavia	My dear, this is Verruca Street Church of England Primary School, not the Royal Shakespeare Company! Your production may not have been technically faultless, but the children have developed enormously, as have you. And that's what matters. You, my dear, are what I said you would be — a success.
Celia	Thank you. But I'm sure the other members of staff wouldn't agree…
Octavia	My dear, it matters not a jot. In return for all the help they didn't give you, I've arranged a few little — let's call them challenges — for the coming term. There should be personal development opportunities for everyone! *(She winks.)*
Celia	Good heavens! They won't know what's hit them!
Octavia	Too true they won't, my dear. And there's a special treat for you, too.
Celia	Yes?
Octavia	I'd like you to direct next year's Nativity play as well! *(The Lights go down on all but Celia; she goes back into her silent scream routine from Scene 1. Then she suddenly snaps out of it.)*
Celia	Oh, all right then. *(Celia and Octavia join the children in a last rousing chorus of "We Wish You A Merry Christmas".)*

End

Other plays by Geoff Saunders

Hanging in There
Ring Ring
Three Short Plays
Under the Rainbow

Printed in Great
Britain
by Amazon

32376808R00037